Go up and down with the roller coaster.

End

I

Follow the explorer through the cave.

End

Help the car finish the race.

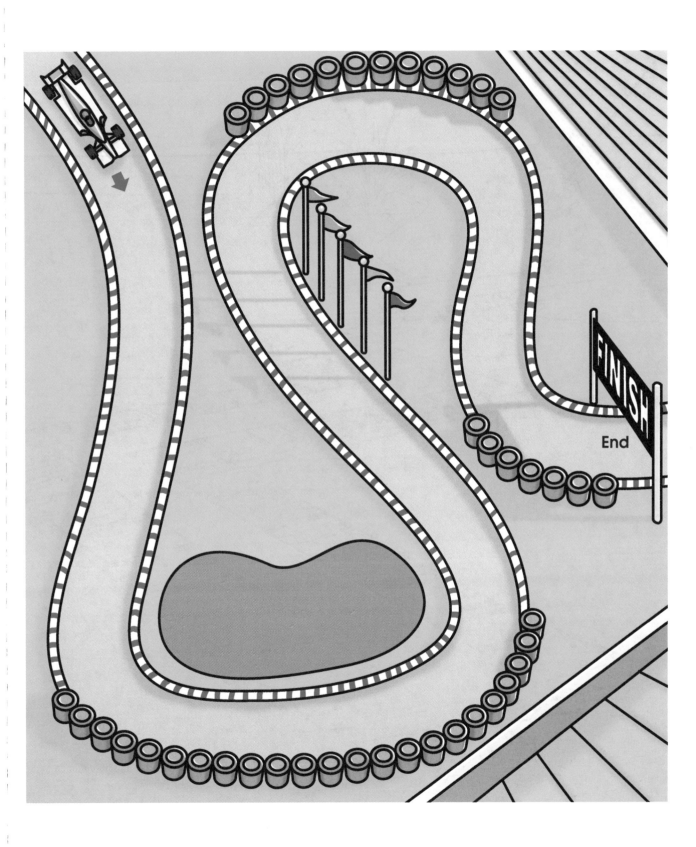

End

# GOING FISHING

Help the fisherman get to the end of the dock.

End

Help the ant get through the tunnel.

End

Help the rocket find its way through space.

End

Help the frog hop across the lily pads.

End

Follow the taxicab around the city.

End

# THE OCEAN DEEP

Follow the submarine through the water.

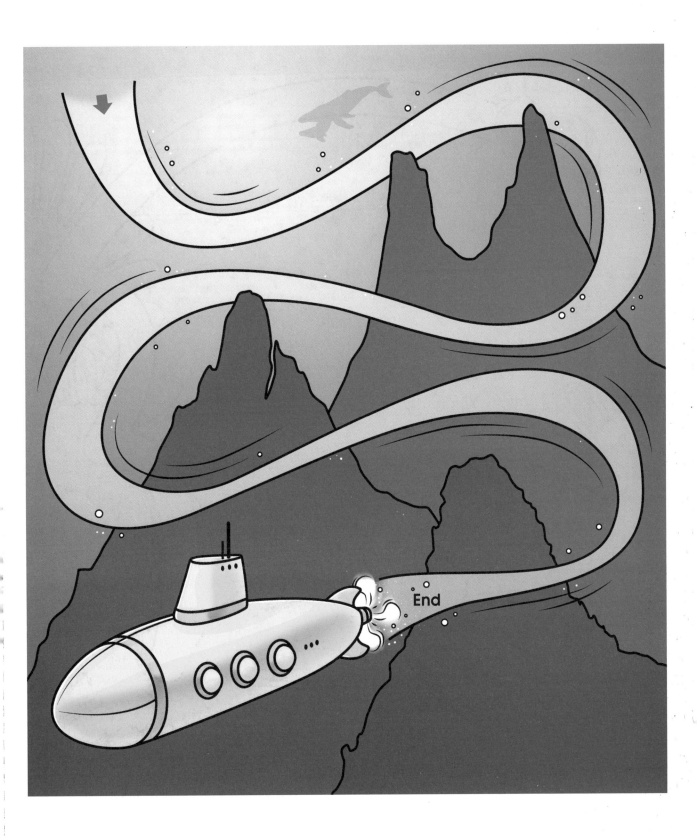

End

Help the bee get from flower to flower.

End

Help Jack climb down the beanstalk.

End

Follow the airplane as it makes shapes.

End

Get to the center of the lollipop.

Help Charlie get to the first floor.

End

# OUT ON A LIMB

Help Scotty Squirrel get to his acorn.

End

Help Jacob through the dark to get to the basement light.

Help the bird find the nest.

End

Follow the path to reach the clam.

End

Get to the center of the web.

End

Help the baker put the cookies in the blue box.

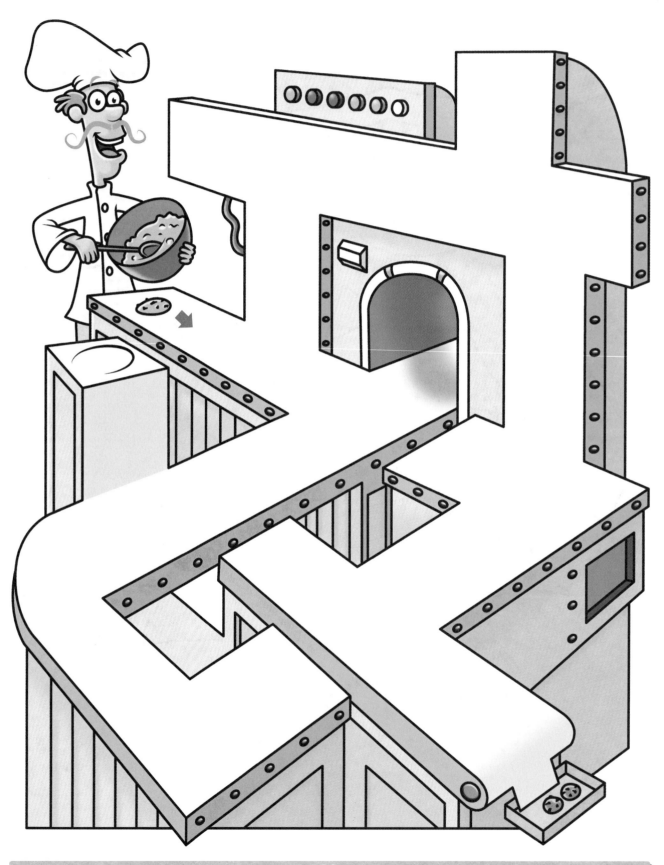

20

Help Simon Seahorse swim to his friends.

Help the chicken cross the road.

Help steer the gondola to the dock.

Help Tommy Turtle get to the pond.

# JUST VISITING

Help the alien get back to the spaceship.

Help the boy run past the skunk without getting sprayed.

End

Help Buzzy Bee return the book on time.

# IT'S SNACK TIME!

Help Randy Rhino get to the bananas.

Help Little Bo Peep find her lost sheep.

Help the cuckoo bird fly back to his house.

Help Donald Dog float to Lazy Lake.

Help get the fork to the meatball.

Help Donna Dinosaur find her babies.

# I SCREAM FOR ICE CREAM!

Help Lucky Lemur get to the ice cream.

# PAINTED PINK

Help Fiona Flamingo get to the paint.

Help Rita Raccoon get to the garbage can.

Help Sammy Snake find his glasses.

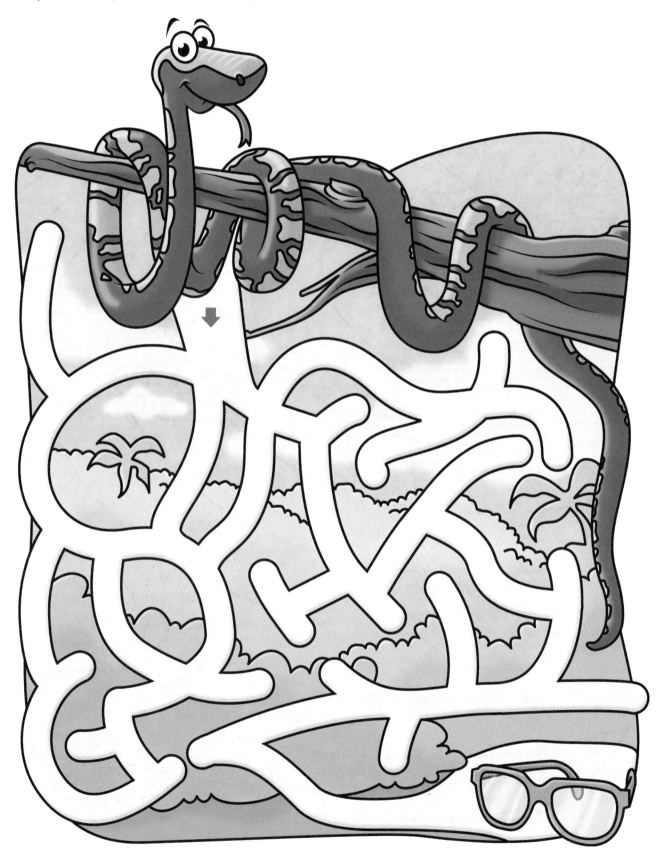

# POND HOP

Help Freddie Frog hop to the lily pad on the other side of the pond.

End

Help Billy Beetle find the house on the lake.

Help Betty Bird fly to her tree.

Help George Giraffe get to Zeb Zebra.

# HIDE-AND-SEEK

Help Daisy Dog find Buddy Bear.

# SUIT UP!

Help Percy Penguin get to his suit.

Help Monty Monkey get to Simon Squirrel.

Help Ron Raccoon get to Felix Flamingo.

Help Bertha Beaver get to her home.

46

Help Peter Porcupine get to his soccer ball.

Help Rex Rhinoceros get to each of his three gifts.

48

Help Mother Hen and her chicks find their home.

Help Sandra Snake slither to the bunch of grapes.

Help Father Fish swim to his babies.

Help Drew Dragon fly to the castle.

Help Larry Lion get to his cub.

Help Sabrina Seagull fly to Wally Walrus.

Help Sal Seal get to the bucket of water.

Help Tonya Pterodactyl get to Danny Dinosaur.

# SNOW DAY

Help Ray Reindeer get to Steven the snowman.

Help Bailey Bird fly to the boy.

Help Hannah Hummingbird fly to Marco Moose.

Help Olivia Octopus get to the scuba-diving salamander.

60

Help Wilma Whale swim to Margo Mouse.

Help Pablo Pigeon fly to his feathered friends.

Help Ollie Owl visit Gary Groundhog.

Help Tiffany Turkey find her egg.

Help Benny Butterfly fly to Allie Alligator.

Help Kacy Koala get to Keegan Kangaroo.

Help Finley Fox run across the bridges.

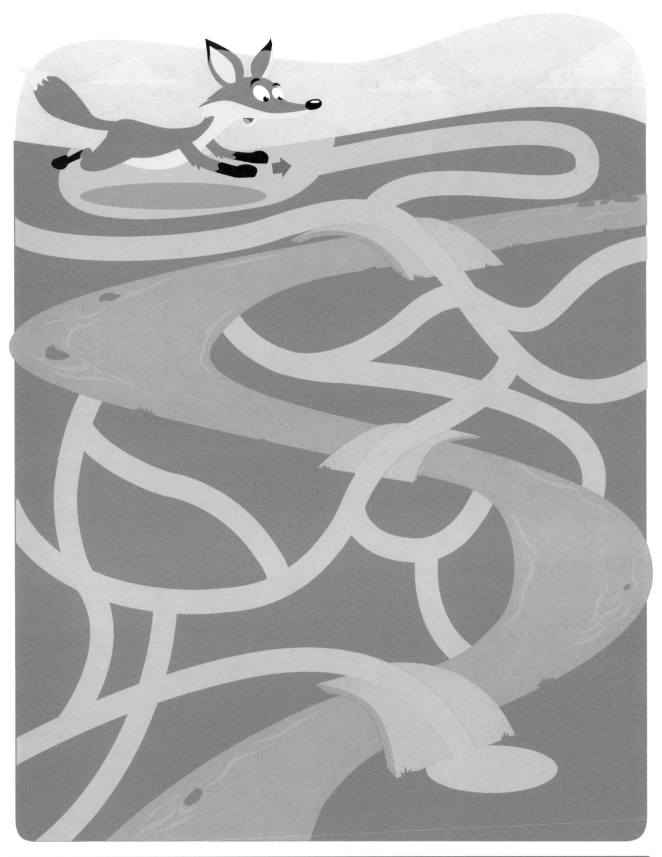

Help Parker Pony gallop to Cowboy Collin.

# DON'T BUG ME!

Help the Maxwell Mantis get to Laura Ladybug.

Help Riley Rabbit visit Haley Hippo.

# MAGNIFICENT MUD BATH

Help Penny Pig join her friend in the mud puddle.

Help Walter Worm get to the book.

Help Renee Raccoon ski to the bottom of the slope.

End

Help the rocket get to the orange planet.

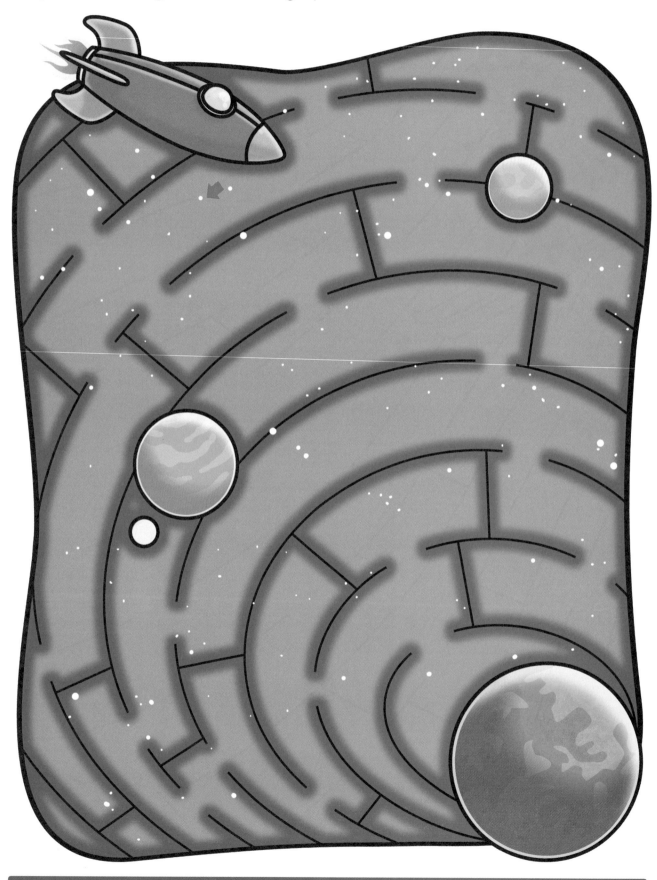

# THAT'S NUTTY!

Help Susan Squirrel get to the acorns.

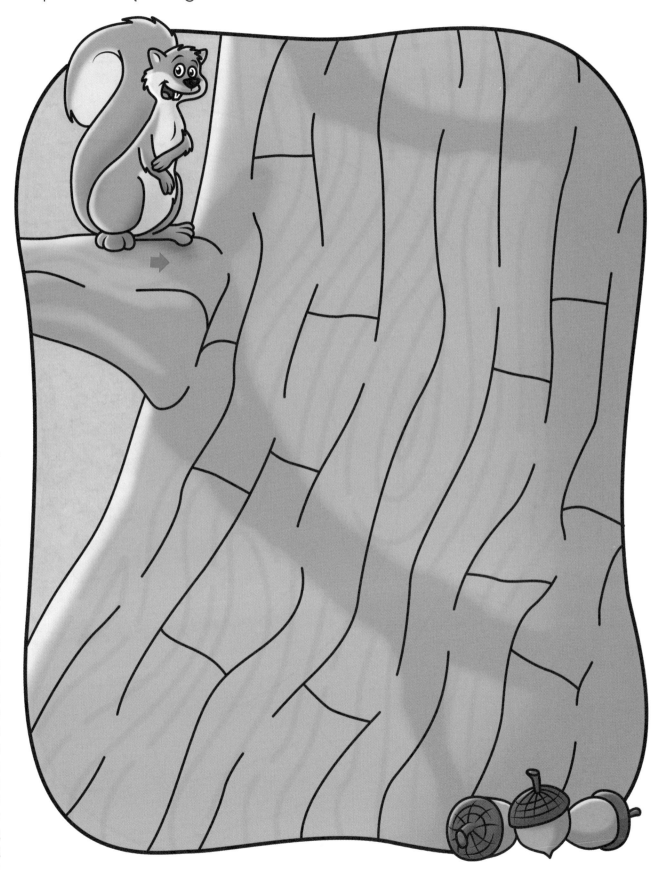

Help Amy Ant and Alexander Ant get to the center of the anthill.

Help the egg get back to its nest.

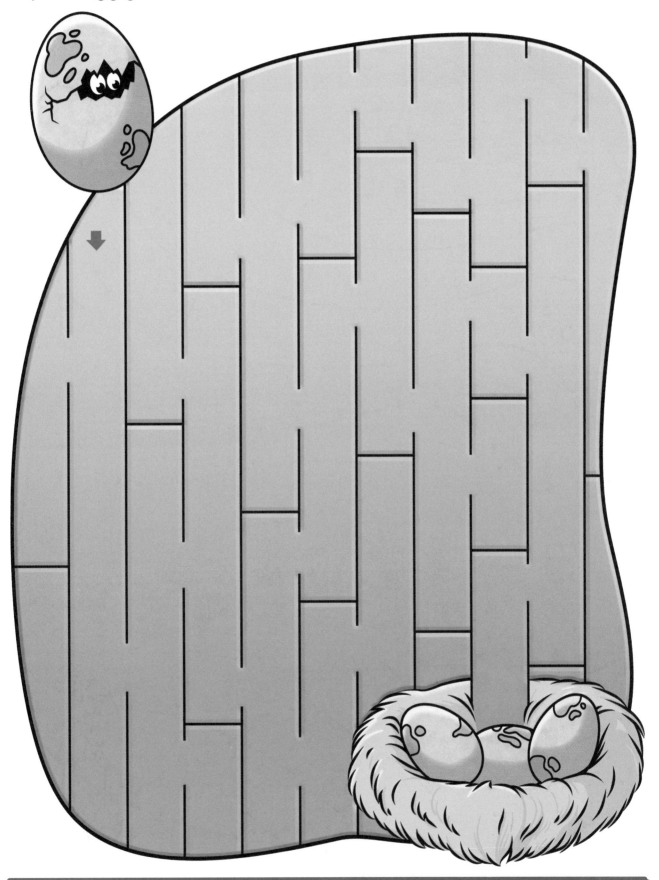

Help Felicity Fish swim to the worm.

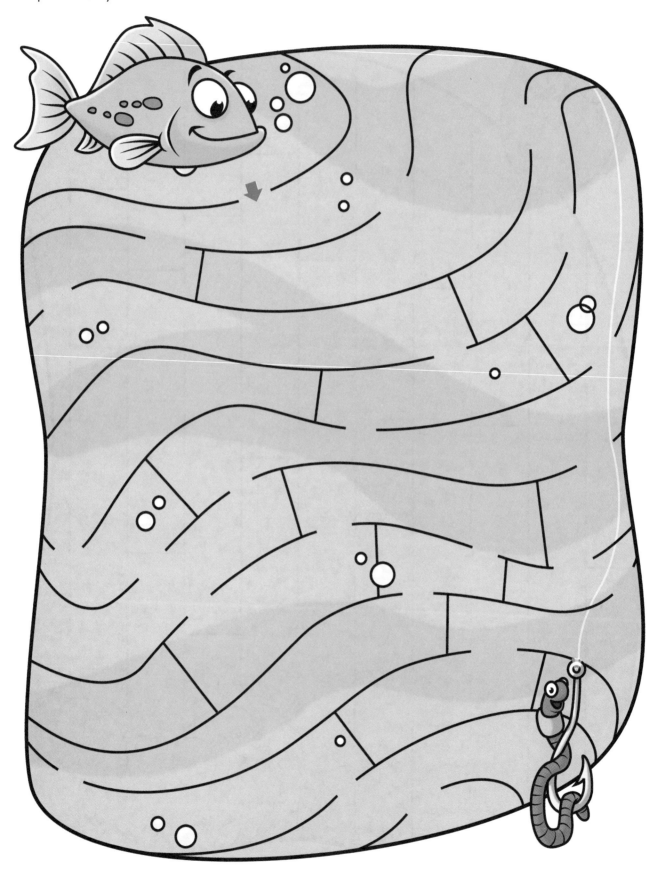

Help Mattie Mouse find the cheese.

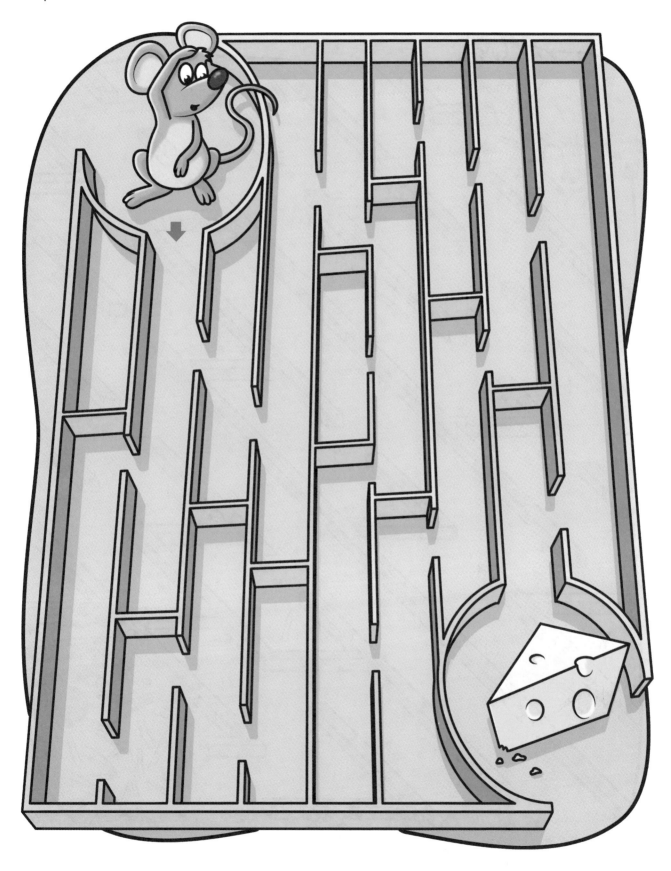

Help Paula Pig get to her dinner.

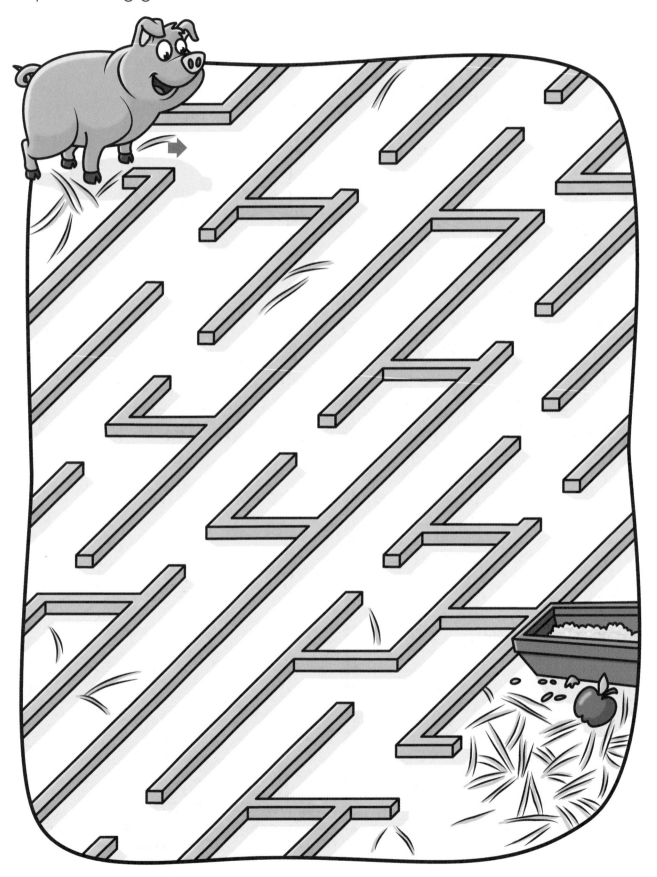

Help the pencil get to the bottom of the page.

Help Barry Bear surf to the beach.

# DESERT OASIS

Help Cory Camel get a drink of water.

Help Monica Monkey swing home to her tree house.

Help Lucy Llama get to the ground.

Help Carrie Cat get down from the tree.

End

Help the helicopter land safely on the landing pad.

End

# FRIENDLY DRAGON

Help the knight get to the dragon.

Help the pirate ship sail to the island.

# PLANETARY RINGS

Help the alien circle the planet to get to the star.

90

# AT THE RACETRACK

Help the race car cross the finish line.

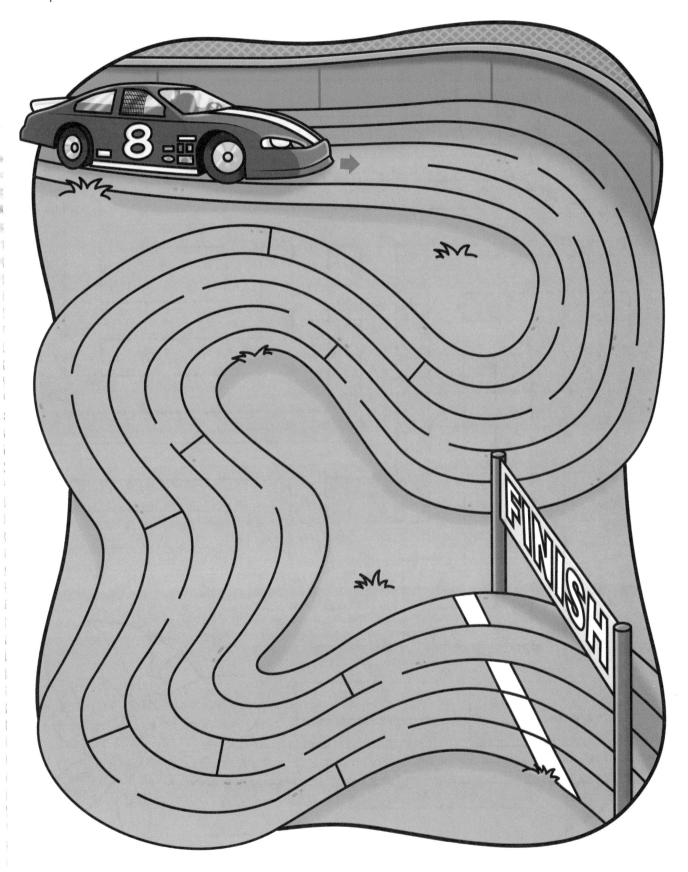

Help Catie Caterpillar get to the butterfly.

# WHERE'S THE WOOD?

Help Bea Beaver get to the forest.

# HOME RUN!

Help the batter run the bases.

# DOWN THE RIVER

Help get to the boat by following the path in the steam.

# DON'T GET CAUGHT!

Help Shawn Shark swim through the net.

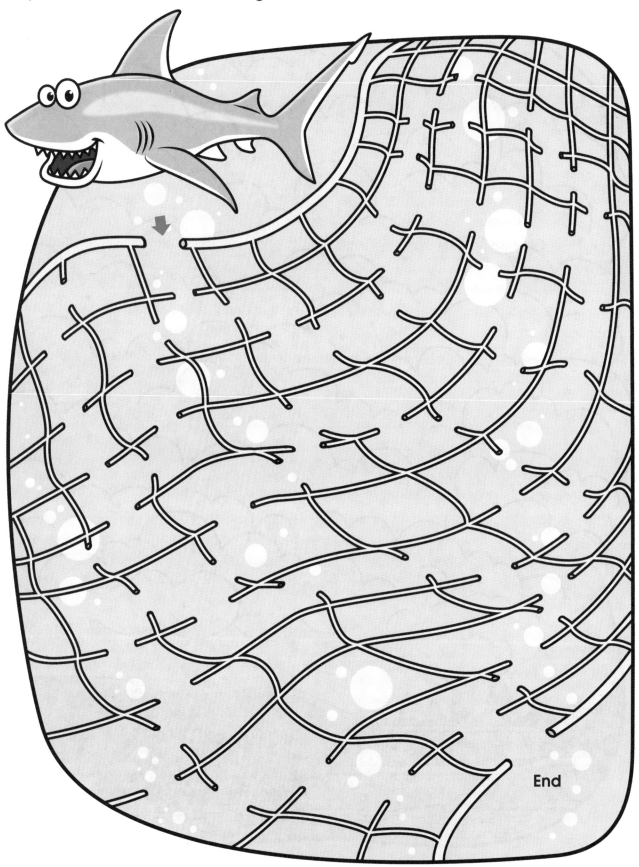

End